Amy Sylvester Katoh

Blue and White Japan

Photographs by Yutaka Satoh

Design by Katharine Markulin Hama

Charles E. Tuttle Company
Rutland, Vermont & Tokyo, Japan

For Yuichi, the sun, Mia, Saya, Tai, and Toshi, the stars, Okasama and Obachama, sister moons, and Edmund Quincy Sylvester, who filled the skies with kites and rockets

No book is written alone. This one is the sum of generous servings of help and cooperation from friends and people we admire who shared their blue and white rooms and collections and recipes without stint. To Sanshiro Ikeda for his blessings, Seiji and Harumi Nibe for creative guidance, Bill and Angela Cruger, Martyne and Tom Kupciunas, Hiroshi and Noriyuki Murata of Kosoen, Chie and Hideki Maegawa, Haruri Ginka Gallery, Mr. and Mrs. Susumu Kakitani, Betty and Gil Hoffman for their consummate hospitality, Henk and Alison Hoksbergen, Tamiko and Tsutomu Makishi, Yasuko and Jissei Omine, Mrs. Yoshiko Shimabukuro of the Daiichi Hotel, Naha, Okinawa, the Matsuda brothers of the Yomitan potters' guild, Sachiko Kinjo, the Kumamoto family of Pension Bisezaki, Katsuko and Shungo Shoji, Hiroyuki Shindo for his indigo inspiration, Kenji and Aiko Tanaka, Yoshihiro Takishita of the House of Antiques for his expertise, Kazuko and Tadashi Morita of Morita Antiques for their knowledge, Yoshichika Kitamura, Chikako and Masanobu Matsumoto of the Gifu Bamboo Society, Shokichi Watanabe and Setsuko Shinoda of Gujo Hachiman, Kibo and Keiko Nomoto, Michiko Natsuhara, Noriko Mikawa, Andrea Heinrichsohn, Kim Schuefftan for his knowledge, Koichi Hama for his calligraphy, Takako Fukuchi and Takako Enokido for their dedication, Hiroko Izumi, Mitsu Minowa for her cooking, Kyoko Machida, Kazuko Yoshiura for her *sashiko*, Reiko Okunushi for her quilts, Paula Deitz for her ikat skies. To you all, and unnamed others, thank you.

Endpapers: *Three hundred and fifty years of Imari. Seventeenth-through-twentieth-century* soba *cups, from the collection of Susumu Kakitani.*
Back of front endpaper: *A treasured Imari plate repaired with silvered lacquer.*
Page 2: *Blue and white welcome. Umbrella stand and old wooden planting frame covered with paper handmade by Kiyomi Tomi of Wajima and painted by Takako Fukuchi. A vintage bedcover of patches over patches is the welcome mat.*
Above: *Imari dish in the shape of Otafuku, a jolly household goddess.*
Right: *Carp and waterfall design with bubbles on a fragment of an old hemp* futon *cover.*
Page 81: *Photo courtesy of La Seine magazine.*

Published by the Charles E. Tuttle Company, Inc., of Tokyo, Japan
with editorial offices at 2-6 Suido 1-chome, Bunkyo-ku, Tokyo 112

LCC Card No. 95-62393
ISBN 0-8048-2052-X

First edition, 1996
First printing, 1997

Printed in Singapore

Contents

Introduction   7

Living with blue and white   15
Entrances   17
Artful doors   22
The best rooms   25
Blue and white details   31
Floor cushions   33
All in the details   37
A fair chair   39
Confessions of a collector   40
Porcelain *hibachi*   46
Bedside manners   51
Yukata   55
A blue and white kitchen   58
Choosing porcelains   65

On the table   71
Blue and white porcelain   73
Japanese porcelain vocabulary   74
A story in a *soba* cup   91
Blue and white skies   97

Indigo threads   99
Indigo textiles   100
Indigo craftsmen   103
An indigo primer   105
Blues in the house   106
The language of design and pattern   109
Choosing old indigo textiles   111
Out of the blue   112
Banner days   117
Tenugui   118

Places, spaces, sources   125

Blue and white vocabulary   128

blue and white Imari porcelains that were staples in the Dutch East India Company's trade with Europe, blue and white have long been the colors Japan has made its name with throughout the world. Today, new combinations and arrangements are constantly being created, but the essential impact of this basic color combination remains as fresh and powerful as it first was thousands of years ago.

The objective reasons for my love of blue and white are easier to explain than the subjective ones. When I first arrived in Japan, fresh out of college, I was struck by the constant presence of these colors. The blue and white aesthetic was one I had  grown up with in Massachusetts, and it made me feel instantly at home when I found it repeated everywhere in Japan. Craftsmen responded to the natural world around them with blue and white creations in textiles and ceramics. From *futon* quilts and cotton kimono, to bowls and plates and porcelains of all kinds, many of the things I used each day were blue and white. Blue and white seemed to surround me and invite me to stay. But it wasn't just an aesthetic attraction. **Most appealing was** the fact that blue and white was the basic color combination of ordinary life. Not of fancy, sophisticated Japan, but of down-to-earth Japan. It was the *tenugui* hand towel. It was the last thing worn at night, the crisp, comforting *yukata* robe slipped on after the bath. Blue and white recurred at every level of daily human activity. Craftsmen pulled on indigo

workclothes to perform  their labor. Men and women in the fields wore baggy

indigo trousers and short wrapped jackets. Workmen tied cotton hand towels

dyed in simple blue stenciled designs around their heads or tucked them

into their belts. Although a haughty, aristocratic blue and white was visible in the most

precious porcelain platters and bowls, the blue and white that caught my twenty-year-old eye was the

homely blue and white of everyday Japan. The no-big-deal teapots hanging from nails in the rafters of

neighborhood crockery shops. The plates and cups of every shape and size that overflowed a table to

serve even a simple breakfast. Blue and white dishes were so commonplace, no one thought twice

about the luxury of using them unsparingly, though I used to despair when it was my turn to wash.

Handmade crafts were one of the few things old, frugal Japan had in profusion. Human

effort and unmatched craftsmanship compensated for a lack  of

resources and natural bounty. With dextrous hands, craftsmen produced

dishes and cloth for daily living that they colored blue and white. From about

the sixth century in Japan, indigo was domesticated and used to dye cloth. Cobalt underglaze-

decorated porcelain was already well developed by 1700. Artisans used blue against the absence of

blue (white) to  create basic patterns, distillations of larger motifs in nature that were

masterpieces of design. When I came to Japan thirty years ago, it

was another time, another country. Today's high-tech, fast-paced society ignores old

traditions. The knowledge of how to create some of the intricate patterns found in antique textiles is

being lost. The soft colors on porcelain bowls of long ago are rarely found on new pieces sold in

department stores. The blues are harsher now, the whites too white. Many of the craftsmen I used to

visit are gone, and their sons do not want to learn the old techniques. And yet — the economic

doldrums of the 1990s may provide a way for Japan to find itself again. As the country comes to terms

with the limitations of growth, it is beginning to reconsider and rediscover what is real, what is precious,

and what is quintessentially Japanese. To me, blue and white is Japan. Though

these colors occur elsewhere, the Japanese response to blue and white  is original and

inspired. It pervades crafts and arts and daily life in a way that is found in no other

country. As such, blue and white Japan is worth searching out and celebrating.

Most of all, it is worth trying to capture its magic in our houses and living spaces today.

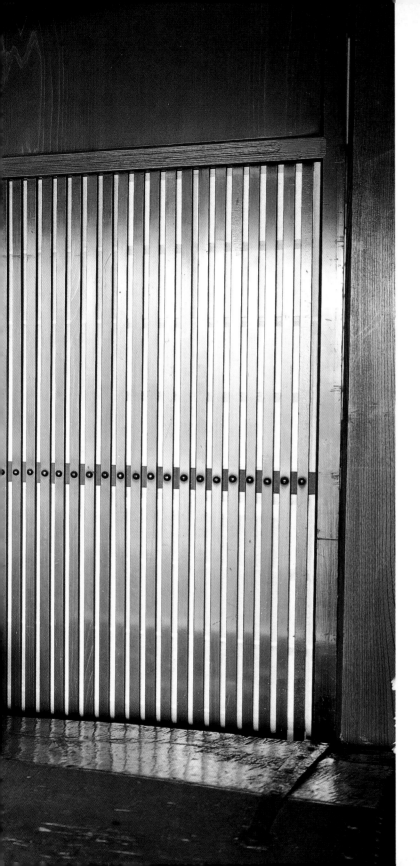

Living with blue and white

means the focus is on simplicity. Here, peace prevails in the entrance-way of the Sanshiro Ikeda house, moved from Toyama Prefecture twenty-five years ago and faithfully restored in Matsumoto. The lines of the alternating slats of dark wood on the sliding door are repeated in the bamboo pattern of the hemp-fiber *noren* curtain created by the late Keisuke Serizawa, stencil designer, dyer, and Living National Treasure. On the massive chest are an old quilt and a *furoshiki,* wrapping cloth.

Entrances

Entrances not only welcome visitors, they also reflect the taste of those who live within. They are considered the face of the home. What better place to introduce a blue and white sensibility? Blue and white has its own energy and it conveys a message of simplicity and order. Start with basic materials — an Imari umbrella stand, a favorite porcelain *hibachi* brazier, some antique textiles — then use them in fresh ways to add texture and character to otherwise anonymous spaces. Try wrapping a basket of flowers and branches in an old *futon* cover of patched indigo. Add a touch of whimsy to an entranceway floor with an arrangement of ragweave sandals and heavy workman's footwear. Consider using *noren,* the split curtains traditionally hung in shop doorways, to delineate space and serve as creative door dressing. Then, in the Japanese way, change them with the seasons: sheer fabrics for summer, thick cotton indigo in cold weather. The entrance is a place to make a statement about what you love and what gives you energy. Share that energy with all who enter by making it an expression of your individuality. Blue and white is the message. The entrance is the place to communicate it.

Left: Rags and riches fill the entrance of the Kupciunas house. Calligraphy on a scroll of *washi,* Japanese handmade paper, by Naoaki Sakamoto of Paper Nao. The ragweave slippers are from Wajima. A Thai horse looks on.
Below: Wooden puppet's feet, workman's footwear, and old ragweave sandals join forces.

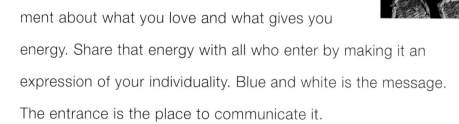

Left: A floor-to-ceiling indigo bamboo grove with openings cut for arrangements of hydrangeas in front of a sculpted concrete staircase and a child's kimono.

Below: Harumi Nibe, in a tie-dyed indigo hat by Ryoko Kodama, greets guests with her Labrador, Tokiwa Gozen. Next to her, a blue and white hemp curtain fragment draped over a freshly cut bamboo lintel serves as a new take on traditional *noren*. Transplanted to Tokyo from Shikoku, Nibe-san is a flower and food artist who brings the rich flavor of country sensibilities to whatever she does. Her style is imbued with the Japanese appreciation for rustic and natural things.

Above: Gossamer *noren* cover a storage cupboard in the display room of Kosoen, an indigo dyer's workshop in Ome, Tokyo. Above the cupboard, a rice-straw bale of fermented indigo sits next to rolls and skeins of undyed cotton thread. On the floor, an old back basket filled with lilies. In the next room are the indigo vats.
Right: A converted temple in Sakakitamura, Nagano, is home, workplace, and showroom for Kibo and Keiko Nomoto, potter/indigo dyer and textile artist respectively. Provisions for going out include an indigo traveling coat, paper umbrella, and covered clogs. Keiko Nomoto's own indigo patchwork collage brightens the wall.

Artful doors. Handsome

definers of space that invite us to enter a house or a room, *noren* can also turn a doorway into a frame for a fluid work of textile art.

Noren are usually dyed with indigo and made of cotton, and sometimes of hemp. They are suspended from a bamboo pole across the front of traditional Japanese shops, where they serve to announce both the name and crest/symbol of an establishment and that it is open for business. When the shop is closed, the *noren* is removed.

In the eighteenth and nineteenth centuries, streets were lined with shops whose vibrant *noren* were a compelling testament to the dyer's art. While modern stores do not usually hang *noren* above their entrances, enough *noren*-graced doorways still exist to offer practical art opportunities to indigo dyers and designers who seek a canvas on which to exhibit their talents.

Above: *Noren* in banana fiber and indigo, spun, woven, and dyed by Toshiko Taira of Okinawa, who has led the movement to preserve the ancient craft of banana-fiber textiles, *bashofu*.
Right: Tie-dyed indigo *noren* hanging in the doorway of the Kakinoki antique shop in Tokorozawa.
Facing page: Sheer magic. An appliquéd *noren* of indigo mosquito netting by Kazuko Yoshiura.

The best rooms

have a certain serenity and clarity of purpose. To the Japanese way of thinking, a main room where guests may visit has to be versatile and beautiful. It should also provide a feeling of well-being. Translated into a Western setting, this means the sort of uncluttered living room where you can put your feet up if you feel like it, throw a party when the spirit moves you, or just sit quietly by the window and daydream, yet always feel refreshed and sustained by things you love. Nestled on a hill in Okinawa overlooking the East China Sea, the room at left meets all these criteria. It is a living room where one is meant to live simply and well. The ever-changing blue and white of sea and sky are an evolving mural, so furniture and other decorative elements have been reduced and downplayed. Instead, the soaring windows provide a spirited sense of place through the use of local craftsmanship in the construction and the addition of blue and white Okinawan textiles and ceramic accents. Used in tandem with other things, blue and white lends a room a relaxed elegance, making it a room to remember.

Left: Straw cushions on the bay-window seat are favorite spots for tea. *Shisa,* temple dogs or lions, by Joga Shima, and a large blue and white covered bowl by Kyoshi Matsuda are dwarfed by the massive wall of local travertine in the fireplace.
Below: A pile of antique textiles waiting to be used.

Left: Country blues and whites in a mountain house in Kobuchizawa. Stretched along the sofa back is a 19th-century horse trapping. Quilted pillows in homespun cotton by Kazuko Yoshiura add comfort. An old, checkered fighting-dog blanket from Shikoku is under the table. Dogfights are now outlawed.

Above: Mood indigo in Haruri Ginka Gallery in Kawagoe. Under beams hung with dyed mosquito netting, a mysterious wooden llama sculpture by Hideki Maegawa shoulders an old *yukata* robe made of patched *tenugui* hand towels, while overseeing other whimsical Maegawa creations: tables and benches of old ships' timbers and other found objects, which he uses to create original furniture for living and laughing.

Above: A quirky sculpture by Seiji Nibe and a banner with a design of carp climbing a waterfall, a traditional symbol of strength and bravery, add panache to the entranceway of an apartment.

Right: A living room that welcomes friends to sit down, relax, and share stories among the owners' favorite things — books, family photos, rustic New England footstools, and, of course, blue and white pillows and floor cushions. The lamp on the right is by Isamu Noguchi. An indigo patchwork quilt does double duty as a rug, and a large lacquered tub, bought at a flea market years ago, serves as a coffee table.

Blue and white details

Simple things well arranged offer quiet inspiration. It is on details that the eye lingers — the enigmatic blue of a long striped textile against a sand-colored wall, the velvety white of a flower in a small Imari vase, the contrast of a checkered textile against richly worn wood. There is no substitute for attention to details in the creation of understated, relaxed style. Using blue and white ceramics that are more lovely than priceless, textiles that have individuality and charm above pedigree, adds intriguing character to a house. For fine-art devotees, imperfection is a flaw, but for those who love Japanese blue and white, a neatly mended antique cloth and a chipped plate carefully repaired and handed down through generations have stories to tell. They are intriguing because their lumps and bumps and mends reveal they are truly valued and cherished. Living with such objects is a joy. A tray of mismatched sake cups, a collection of porcelain shards, a favorite basket of fabric bits and pieces — all of these will brighten a room and evoke a warm response. A Japanese blue and white textile or ceramic has its own integrity, yet it interacts harmoniously with other objects and gives nourishment to all.

Left: 18th-century Japan in the 20th-century folk-art museum house of Sanshiro Ikeda, collector of furniture and crafts from Japan, England, and Korea. Here, a child's oak school desk and chair, an Imari vase, and a striped indigo textile with a family crest form a serene still life.
Below: A contemporary bamboo basket from Shiga Prefecture filled with blue and white ceramic scroll ends.

Floor cushions

No house in Japan should be without
zabuton, versatile floor cushions that
can create an instant seating area and
then be stacked away once guests
depart. *Zabuton* are traditionally filled
with kapok or cotton padding.

Above: *Zabuton* covered in blue and white
kasuri, ikat or patterned cotton, and
modern textile adaptions of old indigo
designs in between.

Left: Calligraphy practice on an
antique glass-covered basket among
scattered *zabuton* covered in vintage
kasuri patterns. A ragweave farmer's vest
in blue and white with red accents waits to
be slipped on as the afternoon grows
cooler. On the table, the dish and brush
holder are old Imari, while the teapot and
cup are contemporary.

Above: A giant red carp splashes up from a colorful textile on the sofa in the Hoksbergen living room. In front, a clever table constructed of lunch delivery boxes and glass. Below, a clouds-and-waves porcelain hibachi features a playful dragon.

Right: Something old, something new around the *irori,* a sunken open hearth, in a Yamanashi country house. The splendid heart-stopping cushions of indigo crosses on white hemp are by Takumi Sugawara, perhaps the most original *tsutsugaki,* freehand design, textile artist working today.

All in the details.

Japan, blue and white and otherwise, is an aggregate of details. Fine lines in small places, moods, moments. Focus with a Western eye on the grand picture and you may miss the quiet corners where the Japanese eye for particulars shines through. Look at the unheralded surfaces: the plasterer's roof gable, the tatami edging, the electrical outlet, the brush stroke on a piece of porcelain, the worn grain of a wooden tray. Peek at the under-kimono if you can. That is where the spirit is revealed.

Above: Handmade blue and white rope in an open-weave basket.

Left, from top: Maple leaves on an Imari plate; sake pourers and cups on an old wooden tray; porcelain umbrella stand with design of banana leaves; flowers, textiles, and odds and ends of porcelain waiting to be arranged for a shoot.

Facing page, clockwise from top: Waves and carp plaster design by Hitoshi Kutsukaki on a roof gable in a Karuizawa house; stone gods on ragweave *obi* sash; a striped horse rein used as edging for tatami; Meiji-era (1868–1912) glass lamp shade and Imari electrical fixture at Kakinoki Antique Gallery.

37

attracted. I spent a luxurious day in Kyoto recently looking for textiles, something I hadn't done for a long time. I visited old friends, a few of Kyoto's textile dealers. Among their fine pieces, nothing really had the spark I was looking for. I went to the pre-auction exhibition of the semi-annual textile sales and poured over my choices from the catalogue. An amusing indigo elephant, quiet soft colors, outlandish proportions and details done by a textile artist who had surely never seen an

Right: Rabbits rampant. Wood, porcelain, clay, and bronze rabbits, gathered on an old storehouse door, impress by numbers, as well as by variety of medium and design.

Right: A calligrapher's collection of brushes hung on a miniature stand is used by Alison Hoksbergen for her ink painting. An Imari teapot and other treasures are stored in the small *tansu* chest.

Below: A trio of antique blue and white *hibachi* used for growing water lilies in the garden.

Porcelain *hibachi*, traditional Japanese

charcoal braziers used for warming hands and rooms, are not easy to collect these days, as good ones are becoming scarce. But fine examples occasionally can be found in antique shops and at flea markets. *Hibachi* were once a luxury item for the upper classes, but as charcoal became readily available in the seventeenth century, wooden *hibachi* with copper liners appeared in ordinary households. When Japan's porcelain industry expanded during the Meiji Restoration, porcelain *hibachi* became popular, especially those hand-painted by Kyushu craftsmen in blue and white patterns.

Later, stencil techniques were used to speed up production and meet growing consumer demand. *Hibachi* are both charming and practical, whether used as intended as braziers or given a new lease on life as flowerpots, table supports, or homes for goldfish.

Above: International bottle convention on the window sill of Harumi Nibe's kitchen. Italian, French, and Japanese bottles, blue and otherwise, create a translucent sparkling tableau.

Right: A collection of blue and white water droppers nestles on an Okinawan silk scarf spun and hand-woven by Tamiko Makishi.

Left: Spiral designs on a collection of sake cups and pourers call for another round!

Below: Blue and white *soba*-noodle cups and flowers in the drawers of an old medicine chest at the Hoksbergen residence. On top, Imari vases stand in front of a proverb painting by Koji Ikeda.

Bedside manners.

As any designing woman or man will tell you, there is no reason not to have fun in the bedroom. Owning a blue and white textile or ceramic is not enough. To experience the true joy of your find, the new piece must have its place in your interior life. Adding well-loved textiles or ceramics to bedrooms brings personal style and taste into private havens. Family mementos, field grasses bursting from a *hibachi,* photos and books, all create an atmosphere of well-being. A much-loved antique quilt is a dear friend and a joy to wake up with each morning. Blue and white cushions add spice to sleeping quarters. A four-poster bed swathed in *yukata* fabric can become a one-of-a-kind place to dream. Old textiles found at flea markets are often fragments with tears and parts missing. They find new life when recycled as unique and spunky pillows, or patched or woven together into an unusual rug. Larger pieces — a still-intact *futon* cover, a giant indigo *tsutsugaki* square — work beautifully as bedcovers. Try combining Western bedding with Japanese blue and white textiles to create bedrooms that express remarkable individuality and help dreamers to wake up inspired.

Left: A tatami-mat sleeping platform is a private island of tranquility and peace. Surrounded by favorite things, from books to family photos to a crane-motif *hibachi,* and under a large blue and white arabesque-pattern duvet cover, you are invited to dream.
Below: A stack of rectangular cushions covered in *kasuri*-patterned indigo.

Below: The scarecrow by Takako Fukuchi and Takako Enomoto of Blue and White, which won first prize in the East Azabu neighborhood scarecrow competition, wears a blue and white *yukata*. On the daybed, a vibrant appliqué quilt by Reiko Okunushi displays a sampling of patterns found in *yukata* robes. Nearby, a tea box covered with *yukata* fabric is both end table and storage space.

Right: An appliqué quilt of indigo and other colored antique fabrics by Reiko Okunushi adds panache to the guest room of a Tokyo house. The quilt's motif is Otafuku, a jolly goddess of hearth and home. On the side table, a 19th-century bubble-patterned textile exudes faded charm.

Yukata

Yukata are light robes of breezy blue and white designs that have been stenciled onto narrow widths of cotton and then sewn into kimono shapes. Traditionally they were worn as robes after the bath to absorb moisture, but today that use survives mainly at hot-spring resorts. Most Japanese now wear *yukata* as summer kimono that are cool and comfortable. Not only the lightness and breathability of the cotton, but the psychological refreshment of the blue and white combination makes the wearer feel cool, even though the garment is long and full-sleeved.

Even today, Tokyo is the center of *yukata* production, inspiring hundreds of new patterns each year with its smart sense of style. (New patterns usually appear in department stores as summer draws near, but Blue and White in Azabu Juban features *yukata* fabrics in the latest designs year-round.) Patterns were originally drawn from sources in nature: birds, flowers, trees, animals, landscapes. A study of the history of *yukata* patterns is a study of Japanese graphic design in all its glory: strong, bracing reductions of natural phenomena to designs that can be wrapped around the human torso. This brilliance in reducing things of everyday life to patterns and then adapting these patterns to the human form is one of the high points of Japanese textile design.

Patterns vary for men and women, for young and old. Children's *yukata* have still different blue and white designs. Fashions change in *yukata* patterns each year, but the glory of the blue and white tradition always reaches a peak when people dress in *yukata*, bright *obi* around women's waists and smart tie-dyed sashes tied low around slim male hips, wooden clogs on bare feet, and go out to celebrate summer: fireworks, festivals, and outdoor concerts. The blue and white *yukata* is loved not only for brilliance of design, but also because it is a garment of recreation and fun.

Although techniques in *yukata* dyeing and coloring have become sophisticated and advanced, dyeing is still a labor-intensive process that entails many pairs of hands. And despite refinements and new color schemes, dyers and customers alike always seem to return to the basic combination of dark blue and white.

The *yukata* fabric comes in rolls about 11.8 meters long and 36 centimeters wide, which can be used for any design project calling for textiles. Covered tea boxes, photo albums, picture frames — all look striking in bold blue and white. Quilters have found a new frontier in blue and white *yukata* material as well, producing ingenious new designs and combinations that expand the boundaries of this hard-working textile.

Left: Spiral-pattern *yukata* drying outside at the Nibe house. On the floor, a pair of padded indigo slippers awaits the laundress.

Right: A New England four poster transplanted to a Tokyo house is dressed up with variously patterned lengths of blue and white *yukata* cotton. An assortment of cushions and an early 20th-century festival jacket with a design of tied paper fortunes provide a fresh contrast to the lace coverlet.

Previous page: A summery linen quilt cover dresses the *futon* bed in the Nibe guest room. A *yukata* has been left out for the guest to slip on, and another hangs on the clothing rack. An ink-painting screen and an arrangement of wildflowers in a ceramic *hibachi* give spirit to the lacquered alcove.

A blue and white kitchen

makes sense. Inside, outside, topsy-turvy at times, it may go from calm to chaos with the regularity of the meals of the day, but behind the scenes the logic of color helps maintain balance and harmony. Blue and white hand towels placed hastily in drawers seem to form themselves into well-ordered stacks; blue and white tiles placed around a stove or sink create an easy order. A cheerful blue sink makes washing up less of a chore. Even mismatched Imari and other dishes piled high in cupboards or towering on counters come together if they are all blue and white.

The kitchen today is more lived in than any other room in a house. This is the place where families and friends gather to cook, talk, and eat. Filling a center of activity with unpretentious Japanese blue and white ceramics creates a calm and order that welcome all who enter. People can be themselves against this nothing-fancy background setting. Best of all, the innate order of the blue and white combination, even in its wildest patterns and pairings, keeps chaos at bay in today's hectic world.

Right: Blue and white bottoms. Clean-up time features the chance to turn over some lovely pieces of Imari — old, new, valuable and not — and see what different chops and marks are painted there. The other side of an Imari plate tells a whole different story. The Imari shards in the old goldfish bowl were found on neighborhood walks.
Below: Everyday family rice bowls. Mends add flavor.

Left: Stacks of blue and white bowls ready for lunch. No need for everything to coordinate. Mix, match, juxtapose, and let the colors clash and patterns crash where they will.
Below: 19th-century crane-shaped plates and sake pourers set out for a small dinner. Behind, a traditional glass storage jar keeps homemade ginger cookies handy.

Above: Surrounded by blue and white dragonfly tiles hand-painted by Kaoru Fujisaka for Tokyo's Blue and White, a four-burner stove becomes an enchanted place to cook.

Right: Chaos in the kitchen! Party preparations mean food, flowers, cooking, decorating, all happening at the same time. Only the theme of blue and white offers calm amid the storm.

Right: Blue and white delight in the specially designed kitchen of Rêves de Vie, the innovative restaurant of Patrice Julien in Tokyo's Centre des Arts Français. Brilliant cobalt-blue stove and refrigerator, made to order in Japan, catch the eye, while the Mexican checkerboard tiles play with it. French and Japanese aesthetics combine in a kitchen whose glory is in its attention to detail. The creator and chef scours flea markets to find ceramics and other accents for the tables, walls, and counters. And everyday, spicy aromas mix with the visual feast to assure the diner of a meal to remember from a blue and white kitchen.

Right: An original dishcloth stitched by Kazumi Yoshida against a backdrop of blue and white porcelain tiles.

Below: Only the best ingredients are used in the kitchen of the Rêves de Vie restaurant, in Tokyo's Shirogane district. Carefully chosen blue and white ceramics and cottons give flavor. Here, a spatter-pattern bowl with a maple-leaf motif, an assortment of tin spoons on a bold blue and white hand towel, and, under the spatula, an unusual crescent-shaped tile.

study it, although, in fact, remarkably little is written about it in English. Korean potters brought blue and white techniques from the mainland to Kyushu at the beginning of the seventeenth century. For a while potters and patrons had to be content with inferior Japanese copies of Korean originals. Just when Japanese potters developed a sense of themselves and diverged from Korean prototypes is uncertain. Orders from Europe originally went to China, where the porcelains were superior, but wars in China brought the business to Japan and resulted in the development of Japanese export ware, blue and white porcelains totally different from those made for the domestic market. While Chinese Ming-dynasty and Korean Yi-dynasty pieces are impressive, something simple and strong speaks out from Japanese porcelains, making them original statements apart from and, to my mind, above their Chinese but close to their Korean antecedents.

What is distinctive about Japanese blue and white porcelain? Themes are straighforward, grasses perhaps, or flowers, waves and birds, images of nature. But the observation is exquisite, the ability to capture a moment on a small curved surface is unparalleled. As collector and dealer Susumu

Right, above: Tools of the kitchen trade fill a convenient small-sized blue and white stenciled *hibachi* with a scene of travelers crossing a wooden bridge. Next to it, a snowflake-shaped tile waits for hot things to be set down.

Right, below: Okinawan pots fresh from the kiln of Tsunehide Shimabukuro.

Below: Lily-pad-shaped tile from an old bathhouse with a bat and autumn grasses motif found at a flea market.

Kakitani has observed, Japanese artists had to have the eye of an ant to be able to fit universal themes and motifs on the side of a small cup. The deft distillation of what they saw around them is the greatest gift of Japanese craftsmen.

Color is also an issue when I choose blue and white. I know this is old-fashioned, and probably due to the fact that when I started collecting, Edo-period (1603–1868) blue and white Imari was readily available, but I prefer lighter, more

The pleasure of blue and white comes from having a piece that fits you and your way of living. Maybe the blue and white plate is the perfect shape for serving your special recipe for ginger pork or chilled tofu, or maybe it holds your correspondence or pins on the bureau. Like a husband or wife, it suits you, and promises a lifetime of enjoyment together.

subtle colors to the brighter cobalt blues of the later nineteenth century. Although these are very popular now, as are the stenciled patterns that became common around the same time, I am drawn to softer colors and less distinct designs because they are more retiring when serving food and don't call for attention like the later pieces. But that is all a matter of taste.

On the table

is where blue and white ceramics truly shine. The simplest fare becomes elegant with the artful use of a few dramatic Imari dishes.

When I set tables, I begin with the tablecloth. This forms the backdrop, the canvas. A clean old bedcover perhaps, in a *karakusa,* arabesque, pattern, or an indigo carrying cloth placed on the diagonal. Serve salad on rectangular blue and white plates, add a casual arrangement of indigo-purple flowers, fill a team of tall glasses with roughly rolled cloth napkins, and even the most basic fare will assume gourmet dimensions.

The Japanese blue and white ceramic tradition was born with the discovery of white porcelain clay (kaolin) in Kyushu, southern Japan, in 1616 by Ri Sampei, a naturalized Korean. Many Kyushu pottery kilns converted to high-fire porcelain production, and with the fall of the Ming dynasty in China in 1644, Dutch traders brought European orders for porcelain to Japan. In a startlingly short time, Japanese porcelain grew highly sophisticated and developed its own distinctive character.

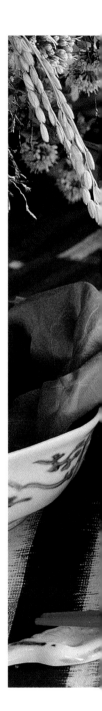

Japanese porcelain vocabulary

Sometsuke is a generic term for blue and white cobalt underglaze porcelains.

Arita is cobalt underglaze porcelain, named after the district where it was first made.

Imari designates underglaze porcelain, originally blue and white, produced in the Arita district on the island of Kyushu from early in the seventeeth century. It is named after the port from which it was sent to other parts of Japan, such as Nagasaki, to be loaded onto Dutch ships headed for Europe. Arita and Imari are largely synonymous.

Shoki Imari, "early" Imari, was made from 1616 to 1650. It is not often seen today.

Ko Imari, "old" Imari, is porcelain of blue cobalt underglaze on a gray-white ground. It can also refer to overglazed, colored enamel porcelains of the time. Produced from about 1650 until 1750, Ko Imari is rare and highly prized today.

Export ware describes Japanese porcelains made to European tastes, ordered by traders of the Dutch East India Company for the European market. These are characterized by bright, enamel colors.

Inban, designs stenciled onto ceramics that were smaller and more detailed than the free, loose designs of hand-brushed pieces, became popular in the second half of the nineteenth century. The Meiji Restoration opened the country in 1868, and new methods to step up production were introduced to meet growing demand for porcelains of every kind, including *hibachi,* which had heretofore been made of wood or metal.

Above: Spotted bowls with red lacquer lids are a family heirloom, a treasure received from a kind and savvy mother-in-law. Sake pourers serve as candle stands.

Left: Old Imari bowls, gathered over many years of collecting, reflect the soft colors of a patched collage of stenciled hemp fabric used as a tablecloth. The piece in front is a small lidded rice bowl.

one has a different plate. If you are worried because a dignified prince and princess are coming for dinner, relax — they'll have more fun if you don't try to live by their rules. Be original. Use your dishes in new ways — pour some dipping sauce for spinach samosas in individual sake cups. Pick some wild chrysanthemums or some autumn grasses and place them in blue and white bottles lined up on the table. Use an old Imari bath tile as a hot plate. If you keep blue and white as the unifying force, aesthetic harmony will prevail. Then feel free to expand and express your own taste and spirit within that blue and white theme. This is the essence of blue and white living.

Above: Teacup irreverently served on stitched country footwear.
Left: Prized antique Windsor chairs around an 18th-century English oak table (all from the Sanshiro Ikeda collection) form a serene backdrop for a Japanese tea party for two. Barley tea and rice balls await on a vintage striped horse rein.

Right: Indigo mosquito netting weaves a spell over an antique Spanish table wrapped in blue and white striped horse textiles. Dishes stacked on the table issue an easy invitation to help yourself and have a good time.
Below: Old Imari sake-cup rests reborn as candle stands.

Above: The simplest meal comes alive with the use of a strong textile, here, a double *kasuri futon* cover.

Left: A grouping of blue and white stacked dishes, a worn roof tile, and antique wooden candlesticks on a *tansu*. The table is reflected in the unusual lacquer mirror with a mysterious carved calligraphy frame, inviting us to join in the meal.

Right: Set a blue and white table and the rest takes care of itself. The job is done here with a *shibori futon* cover spread as a tablecloth and a mix of blue and white dishes. An Imari bowl filed with azaleas is the crowning blaze of color.

Below: Teatime at the Nibe house means interesting food and unexpected combinations of food and dish and cloth.

Left: Amazing grace. Even sandwiches have dignity when served in this timeless room in Sanshiro Ikeda's museum house. Arranged on an old blue and white *sashiko furoshiki* and accompanied by an Okinawan basket (originally for hanging overhead to keep provisions cool and aired), the simplest fare takes on elegant proportions.

Left: Tadayoshi Ikemoto's whimsical teapot with black-eyed Susans sets the tone for lunch outside. A rectangular basket serves as a tabletop.
Below left: Spaghetti squash forms a brilliant contrast against a platter of cobalt blue and white.
Below: Rice served on green leaves is picture perfect.
Right: A spur-of-the-moment lunch at Harumi Nibe's house becomes an affair to remember under a colorful canopy of antique trappings originally used in Tohoku to decorate horses.

Left: Here rustic and sophisticated come together and speak of good taste. A large painting by English artist Lucy Jones and a 17th-century carved wood Burmese Buddha bless a lunch on the run. Fresh flowers repeat the yellow and green accents on an antique French country table set with an old *tsutsugaki* textile with a pattern of *noshi,* folded paper used to decorate a gift.

Above right: An arabesque-pattern *furoshiki,* the textile predecessor of the paper bag, becomes a cheerful picnic blanket on an enchanted Okinawan beach.

Above: Served on a handmade Okinawan basket, simple fare makes a memorable alfresco picnic created with sun, sea and thee, blue and white.

Right: Blue and white bubbles over on this table set for a festive dinner party. Stripes and spots combine close to the boiling point, but never explode as they would were it any other color combination. Old Imari plates, new plates, two contrasting *kasuri* textiles overlaid as tablecloths, and new tie-dyed napkins create layer upon layer of blue and white. The wildflowers were arranged by Harumi Nibe. The room is enclosed by *shoji,* Japanese paper screens, on three sides. In the background hangs a 17th-century Genji-Heike battle screen.

Previous page: On the veranda of a converted temple in Matsumoto, a spontaneous picnic of what is available has more energy than anything long planned and elaborately staged. Rags and baskets and blue and white make the difference.

Right and below: In the garden of Kosoen, lunch on the ròcks. Free-flowing indigo textiles and wine chilling in a small *hibachi* add to the exuberance that indigo and a blue and white sky can create.
Standing on guard is a low-fired clay pig incense burner, used to discourage insects.

Blue and white skies

need to be celebrated. Call some friends, run to the local market, and think simple. For a picnic outdoors, the key is in the presentation, which should be casual and unfussy. If food is served on blue and white platters among comfortable textiles spread out on the deck — small indigo patchwork quilts, an old blue and white checkered dog blanket, a large ragweave rug — the picnic will shine. Scatter some leaves from nearby trees on the plates or arrange them in hand-painted paper lanterns. For a crowning touch, stretch a gauze indigo-dipped canopy overhead to shade the revelers below.

Left, below: Friends and family gather on the deck to enjoy a blue and white lunch. Above, indigo-dyed gauze reflects the color of the sky and protects from the relentless sun. Below, blue and white *zabuton* help make an impromptu picnic a party to remember.
Clockwise from top left: Even an old blue and white dog blanket works as a tablecloth; Imari bowls and platters filled with simple summer food; a ceramic incense burner for mosquito coils; hand-painted paper lanterns by Takako Fukuchi of Blue and White; grilled sausages accented with green leaves; dessert stacked in an old two-tiered basket.

Indigo threads

Some mornings seem to come directly from the indigo pot. Pale blue washes of sky running down to triple-dipped indigo mountains. In the garden of Kosoen in Ome, Tokyo, newly dyed cloths — bolts of inky blue, fresh from the indigo vats — mimic the colors of the morning. The pot design on the large *noren* in the center is the dyer's logo.

Indigo textiles were the fabric of the country-

side in Japan, created from a life in close harmony with mountains, valleys, and seas. Rugged, durable kimono and work clothes were made of what was available, first bast fibers, hemp, barks, grass, and tree fibers. When cotton was introduced, around the fifteenth century, that warmer, softer fiber became the fiber of choice for spinning, weaving, and dyeing.

Once there was a loom in every farmhouse and fisherman's cottage. Each household created its own clothes, quilts, towels. Farmers harvested indigo from the fields, and frothy indigo-dye vats were a common sight. From today's affluence, we look back and see that the beauty of those blue textiles was born from the hard ground of poverty. People then had no choice but to make do as they could. Today, choice is the opiate of the people, and the techniques that remain do not have the strength born of necessity and hard work that shone in the old indigo compositions. Bits of brilliance still remain in *yukata* patterns and the works of stencil and tie-dye dyers. But where is the lyricism of the nineteenth-century textiles? I keep going back to flea markets and antique shops, because it's those old textiles that speak most eloquently.

Right: The hands of Shokichi Watanabe of Gujo Hachiman in Gifu show different stages of his craft, from tying the cloth in knots to resist the dye, to hanging out his newly dyed *shibori,* to dipping the cloth to be dyed, and undoing the knots.
Below: Dried indigo waiting to be used.

The language of design and pattern

Pattern is everywhere in Japan. The curve of a leaf, the swirl of a wave, spots of rain, the sway of bamboo, all are reduced to their essence to embellish the surface of textile, ceramic, metal, or paper. Many patterns used in Japan come from Korean or Chinese antecedents, but the lyrical Japanese observation of nature, the keen eye for the fleeting moment, the delight in detail, allow craftsmen to capture and transpose nature's motifs into designs of unique eloquence that set the patterns of Japan apart.

Once you begin identifying patterns in one medium such as cloth or clay, you will recognize them across the Japanese craft spectrum. Turtles and waves, pine trees and cranes, plum blossoms, checks, stripes, lightning, clouds, and the like form the common art vocabulary of the entire country. They all are traditionally associated with meanings and stories, which were close to folklore. Many of the most popular motifs are also auspicious: for example, giant radishes (fertility), bamboo (longevity), and rice (fecundity). Other patterns with implied messages are chrysanthemums, peonies, butterflies, dragonflies, bats, and the twelve Chinese-zodiac animals, each with its own characteristics.

Decoration by Japanese craftsmen has reached heights unsurpassed anywhere in the world, yet letting materials themselves speak, without added embellishment, is also given as much admiration as decoration. In the language of Japanese pattern and design, it is the freshness of approach that matters.

Left: A *tsutsugaki* of long-living tortoises shares good fortune with visitors to the Hoksbergen house, with a carving of three monkeys who speak, hear, see no evil.
Right, from top: Pattern parade. Indigo textile with alternating bands of fine pattern, including chrysanthemums and water; lion's hair; blue and white checks; swimming carp.

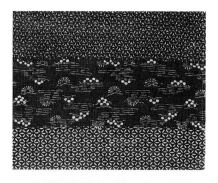
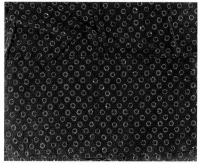

Choosing old indigo textiles

Words of wisdom from Tadashi Morita of Morita Antiques in Tokyo.

Colors. *Blue:* I don't know why, but Japan seems to avoid bright, basic colors. There are many different shades of blue: reddish, purplish, blackish (which gives the strange impression that the fabric hasn't been used), yellowish, almost-green, pale sky blue. But none is really bright. I prefer washed-out blue, a faded powder blue. Real lovers of antique cloth will look for a touch of white between blue threads.
White: I never pay much attention to white, but when I choose a washed-out blue, the white areas will usually be a dirty white, not pure.
Other colors: In *tsutsugaki,* natural colors are sometimes mixed with chemical dyes.

Design. Look for an interesting design on the textile, one with some charm or power. I prefer floral motifs in *tsutsugaki.* I have never seen a truly top-quality tiger or phoenix. Textile designs are not professional artworks — otherwise they would not be folk art! But even if a piece has been rendered by a folk artist, it can still be a beautiful, collectible work if it has some humor or whimsy to it.

Texture. I prefer thick cotton to other materials, and ideally the threads should be homespun and woven by hand — and dyed by hand, of course.

Age. I judge the age of a textile by experience, so I can't give others a simple formula for how to determine age. But it's useful to remember that while cotton and indigo first came to Japan about one thousand years ago, they were subsequently lost for many centuries. Indigo was originally used only to dye hemp. Cotton was reintroduced to Japan 400 years ago and became popular because it accepts indigo dye readily.

Mending. I don't mind at all if a textile is mended. In fact, patches and mends sometimes give more meaning and feeling to a piece.

Left: Textile art. Sanshiro Ikeda wears a padded sleeping kimono with an auspicious crane and turtle design that invokes the spirituality of the crane and the longevity of the turtle. The masterful interaction of the cranes around the family crest symbol is a brilliant example of an anonymous dyer's mastery of his medium. (A front view of Ikeda-san and the kimono can be found on page 8.)
Below: Keiko Nomoto, a textile and indigo artist and kimono devotee, stitching one of her original *sashiko* pieces.

Out of the blue.

There's nothing like it! The thrill of the hunt at the flea market. The energy of the sudden find. You spot. You bargain. You bring it home. But when you get home with your treasure, you realize you have a smelly blue and white textile or a blue and white ceramic pitted with the dirt of the ages.

So hit the tubs! Man the soaps, the detergents, the bleaches, and the brushes! If it's a cotton or hemp textile, immerse it in cold water with Woolite, or in Japan, Monogen. It can soak for some time while the grime emerges. (But be careful if your textile has other colors present, for they can be fugitive, particularly the volatile reds. Don't let them sit in water for any time at all.) If it is dark indigo and doesn't seem to have been washed before, throw a half cup of vinegar or salt into the cold-water bath to stabilize the color. I like to see the excess indigo cloud the water and swim away, leaving a gentler and deeper blue in the textile. The joy of hanging a newly clean *futon* cover or kimono on the line and watching it dry is indescribable. The original energy and brilliance of the textile have been restored. The richness of usage and mellowness of age deepen with each washing. Threads become distinct, and the

Right: Setsuko Shinoda stops to cool herself at the town well in Gujo Hachiman in Gifu Prefecture. She wears a splashy indigo *yukata* in a Chinese bellflower pattern by Shokichi Watanabe. Hanging above the well is a *shimenawa,* a sacred rope. **Below:** The *noren* of the Hotel Kikunoyu in Matsumoto, Nagano Prefecture, greets all passers-by.

Left: Hung from tall bamboo poles lashed together, a long, heroic Kintaro banner adds drama to a temple meditation tower outside Matsumoto that overlooks the Japan Alps. (Momotaro is a popular mythical boy hero of Japan, known for his strength.)

Right, above: Washday blues. Blue and white laundry drying in the Okinawan sun — kimono, bathing suits, and *shibori* cloths used for everything from carrying picnic provisions to drying children just out of the surf.

Right, below: A design-perfect horse trapping invigorates the concrete of an ultramodern Tokyo house. On the left, a flower arrangement under way in a blue and white porcelain *hibachi*.

texture and depth of the fabric are wonderful to see when they emerge. You have released the textile from years of neglect, and your reward is the pleasure of owning a shining old/new piece imbued with the spirit of the maker who wove or dyed it years before.

Washing is equally satisfying with blue and white ceramics. Take them home and plunge them into a tub of hot water and suds. If normal dish detergent isn't strong enough for the deep dirt, try a cleanser or bleach. This applies only to blue and white porcelains. Polychrome overglaze ceramics must be handled more carefully. Blue and white is all underglaze and so can withstand more robust — but still gentle — treatment. If all the dirt is not removed on the first wash, leave the dishes to soak in hot water and a gentle bleach for as long as it takes to remove the grime. Then pick them up one by one and scrub each vigorously with a soft brush. Some delicacy is required when you wash textiles, but the ceramics can stand a fair amount of persistence.

You will be dazzled by the transformation that has taken place You sensed your treasure's power and potential at the flea market With simple washing, the blues and whites have come clean and the acuity of your eye and rightness of your instinct are confirmed! Freshly scrubbed, your ceramics and textiles sparkle in their brightness and new-found energy. The only thing more satisfying than discovering treasures at the market is bringing them home and returning them to their original splendor with soap and water, a brush, an iron, and care.

Banner days are magical.

May 5 is Boys' Day in Japan and celebrates the sons of the family. An indigo Boys' Day banner hung outside lends an air of excitement to the celebration and announces the season to all. At left, Sanshiro Ikeda celebrates his eighty-sixth birthday with a lively *tsutsugaki* banner. Banners such as this are traditionally used on holidays, festivals, and other special occasions (such as observances at shrines or sumo tournaments) to communicate a message of time and season and celebration. Wraparound banners (rather than the kind that are hung) are used to mark boundaries for gatherings of various kinds, including festivals, funerals, and groundbreakings.

come to recognize their beauty and now sell them as the art-to-wear and art-at-work pieces they are.

As surprising as it is to visitors, this simple length of cloth is also a bath towel — a narrow one, indeed. Most hot springs in Japan give guests a *tenugui*. This is supposed to provide cover as you walk naked into the steaming public bath. Shield whatever parts you choose! One friend cleverly suggested that the best place to put it was over one's head. Once you are in the bath, however, the *tenugui* is your washcloth and brush. Wring it out once you are done, then use it to wipe yourself dry. Remarkable efficiency and conservation of resources, all in one small hand-dyed cloth.

Japan has taught me that no person should ever be without a *tenugui*. You never know when you will need one — to dry your hands in a land without paper towels, to wrap some books or flowers, to wipe your bicycle seat after a rainstorm.

Tenugui are quick to wash and quick to dry, and they become better with use. Well-laundered and worn *tenugui* are far more pleasing than freshly dyed new ones. Use them once and then wash in soap and water or just rinse them out and hang to dry on a windowpane or similar flat place. They will dry flat and need no ironing. The *tenugui* — don't leave home without one!

Left: Blues in the bath, inside and out. Overlooking an ever-changing sea and sky, this bath is a dip in paradise. Soak and dream, and when you're done, a fresh *yukata* and slippers will wrap you in blue and white comfort.
Below: *Tenugui* hung on a small lacquered rack. A rustic beckoning cat waves welcome.

Inside the Kakinoki Antique Gallery

Blue and white
places, spaces, sources

Antiques

Akariya
4-8-1 Yoyogi,
Shibuya-ku, Tokyo
03 3465 5578

Antique John
1-6-33 Higashi,
Kunitachi-shi, Tokyo
0425 76 6330

Antique Market
Hanae Mori Bldg. B1,
3-6-1 Kita Aoyama,
Minato-ku, Tokyo
03 3400 3301

Antiques Hasebeya
1-5-24 Azabu Juban,
Minato-ku, Tokyo
03 3401 9998

Bo Peep
1230 Naganuma-cho,
Hachioji-shi, Tokyo
0426 35 1540

Gallery Hasebeya
3-11-3 Moto Azabu,
Minato-ku, Tokyo
03 3401 8840

Harumi Antiques
9-6-14 Akasaka,
Minato-ku, Tokyo
03 3403 1043

Karakusa
5-13-1 Minami Aoyama,
Minato-ku, Tokyo
03 3499 5858

Kawano Gallery
(antique kimono)
102 Flats Omotesando,
4-4-9 Jingumae,
Shibuya-ku, Tokyo
03 3470 3305
also at:
15 Okinohata,
Yanagawa-shi,
Fukuoka Prefecture
0944 73 0131

Kikori Antiques
Hanae Mori Bldg. B1,
3-6-1 Kita Aoyama,
Minato-ku, Tokyo
03 3407 9363

Kochian
4-323-1 Tomoda-machi,
Ome-shi, Tokyo
0428 22 0997

Kurofune
(John Adair)
7-7-4 Roppongi,
Minato-ku, Tokyo
03 3479 1552

Magatani
5-10-13 Toranomon,
Minato-ku, Tokyo
03 3433 6321

Makotoya
2-39-2 Wada,
Suginami-ku, Tokyo
03 3311 1609

Kathryn Milan
3-1-14 Nishi Azabu,
Minato-ku, Tokyo
03 3408 1532

Morita Antiques
5-12-2 Minami Aoyama,
Minato-ku, Tokyo
03 3407 4466

Nanshudo
5-18-9 Hiroo,
Shibuya-ku, Tokyo
03 3440 7408

Nishikawa Antiques
2-20-14 Azabu Juban,
Minato-ku, Tokyo
03 3456 1023

Okura Oriental Art
(Kenji Tsuchisawa)
3-3-14 Azabudai,
Minato-ku, Tokyo
03 3585 5309

Omoshiroya
(vintage kimono)
101, 1-11-21 Higashi-
machi, Kichijoji,
Musashino-shi, Tokyo
0422 22 8565

Setsu Getsu Ka
Christy Fuji Bldg. 2Fl.,
2-13-2 Azabu Juban,
Minato-ku, Tokyo
03 3452 7536

Galleries and Shops

Beniya
(folk crafts)
2-16-8 Shibuya,
Shibuya-ku, Tokyo
03 3400 8084

Bingoya
(folk crafts)
10-6 Wakamatsu-cho,
Shinjuku-ku, Tokyo
03 3202 8778

Blue & White
2-9-2 Azabu Juban,
Minato-ku, Tokyo
03 3451 0537

Fudoki
5-18-10 Minami Aoyama,
Minato-ku, Tokyo
03 3407 3383

Gallery Mayu
(Yu Kobayashi pots)
1-2-10 Nishikata,
Bunkyo-ku, Tokyo
03 3814 1330

Gallery Shun
Sun Palace Bldg. 1Fl.,
4-2-49 Minami Azabu,
Minato-ku, Tokyo
03 3444 7665

Hanada
(ceramics)
2-2-5 Kudan Minami,
Chiyoda-ku, Tokyo
03 3262 0669

Japan Traditional Craft Center
Plaza 246 Bldg. 2Fl.,
3-1-1 Minami Aoyama,
Minato-ku, Tokyo
03 3403-2460

Kamawanu
(tenugui)
23-1 Sarugaku-cho,
Shibuya-ku, Tokyo
03 3780 0182

Mitsukoshi
(department store)
Ebisu Garden Place,
4-20-7 Ebisu,
Shibuya-ku, Tokyo
03 5423 1111

Noya
(tenugui)
5-12-3 Ginza,
Chuo-ku, Tokyo
03 3541 0975

Savoir Vivre
(ceramics)
Axis Bldg. 3Fl.,
5-17-1 Roppongi,
Minato-ku, Tokyo
03 3585 7365

Sei
(indigo textiles)
Hanae Mori Bldg. B1,
3-6-1 Kita Aoyama,
Minato-ku, Tokyo
03 3407 7541

Silk Lab
2-30-4 Numabukuro,
Nakano-ku, Tokyo
03 3389 4301

Takumi
(craft shop & gallery)
8-4-2 Ginza,
Chuo-ku, Tokyo
03 3571 2017

Toukyo
(gallery)
2-25-13 Nishi Azabu,
Minato-ku, Tokyo,
03 3797 4494

Tsukasa (wild flowers
arranged in antique or
unusual containers)
3-7-21 Ginza,
Chuo-ku, Tokyo
03 3535 6929
also at:
45 Mori Bldg. 1Fl.,
5-1-5 Toranomon,
Minato-ku, Tokyo
03 3431 6801

Uchida
(gallery)
2-8-6 Azabu Juban,
Minato-ku, Tokyo
03 3455 4595

**Yokohama Sogo
Japan Shop**
2-18-1 Takashima,
Nishi-ku, Yokohama-shi,
Kanagawa Prefecture
045 465 2111 ext. 5686

Yoshicho
(blue & white ceramics)
1-11-4 Nishi Azabu,
Minato-ku, Tokyo
03 3402 9480

Antiques Outside Tokyo

Chinpun Kanpun
Iizuka Atsushi,
2511-61 Isshiki,
Hayama-machi,
Miura-gun,
Kanagawa Prefecture
0468 75 0944

House of Antiques
(Yoshihiro Takishita)
2-15-3 Kajiwara,
Kamakura-shi,
Kanagawa Prefecture
0467 43 1441

Kakinoki
(Susumu Kakitani)
212-6 Kita Akitsu,
Tokorozawa-shi,
Saitama Prefecture,
0429 95 0626

Kura 50
(Sanae Imaeda)
Hanado 50, Takaya-cho,
Konan-shi,
Aichi Prefecture
0587 55-3314

**Nakamura
Chingireya-ten**
(antique textiles)
Furumonzen Agaru,
Yamatoji-dori,
Higashiyama-ku, Kyoto
075 561 4726

Noboriya
Kitamura, Yoshichiku
5223 Yamaguchi,
Tokorozawa-shi,
0429 28 2666

Tora Antiques
(Erika Yamada)
1-4-8 Honcho,
Nagaoka-shi,
Niigata Prefecture
0258 39 0602

Galleries, Shops, and Craftsmen Outside Tokyo

Akitsuya
53 Kami Ichi no Machi,
Takayama,
Gifu Prefecture
0577 34 5053

Awagami
141 Kawa-higashi,
Yamakawa-cho, Oe-gun,
Tokushima Prefecture
0883 42 6120

Haruri Ginka
3-3 Saiwai-cho,
Kawagoe-shi,
Saitama Prefecture
0492 24 8689

Hyugaji Folk Crafts
1-16-5 Hiroshima-dori,
Miyazaki-shi,
Miyazaki Prefecture,
Kyushu
0985 22 8338

Kame no i Craft Shop
2633 Oaza Kawakami,
Yufuin-cho, Oita-gun,
Oita Prefecture
0977 853301

Kogensha
(folk crafts)
2-18 Zaimoku-cho,
Morioka-shi,
Iwate Prefecture
0196 22 2894

Kudaka Mingei
(folk crafts)
2-3-2 Makishi,
Naha-shi, Okinawa
098 861 6690

Maekawa, Hideki
(sculptor)
1159-18 Shimotomi,
Tokorozawa-shi,
Saitama Prefecture
0429 43 5741

Moyai Kogei
2-1-10 Sasuke,
Kamakura-shi,
Kanagawa Prefecture
0467 22 1822

**Nomoto, Kibo and
Keiko** (potter and
indigo artist)
Aoyagi, Seichoji,
Sakakitamura,
Higashi Chikuma-gun
Nagano Prefecture
0263 66 3768

Noto Nigyo Washi
Nigyo, Mitsui-machi,
Wajima-shi,
Ishikawa Prefecture
0768 26 1314

Omine, Jissei
(potter)
2653-1 Zakimi,
Yomitan-son,
Nakagami-gun,
Okinawa
0989 58 2828

Tefu Tefu
3 Asaichi-dori,
Kawai-cho,
Wajima-shi,
Ishikawa Prefecture
0768 22 6304

Yu Craft
10-7 Sawai-cho,
Kanazawa-shi,
Ishikawa Prefecture
0762 24 0015

Dyers, Weavers, and Others

Aizen Kobo
Nakasuji-dori,
Omiya Nishi-iru,
Kamigyo-ku, Kyoto
075 441 0355

Kosoen
8-200 Nagabuchi,
Ome-shi, Tokyo
0428 24 8121

Kudaka Mingei
2-3-2 Makishi,
Naha-shi,
Okinawa
098 861 6690

Makishi, Tamiko
1336 Aza Maeda,
Uresoe-shi,
Okinawa
098 877 0518

Matsubara Senshoku Kobo
2-20-7 Matsushima,
Edogawa-ku, Tokyo
03 3651 3729

Takemura Sangyo
106 Kamimurakimi,
Hanyu-shi,
Saitama Prefecture
0485 65 2030

Tanaka, Kenji and Aiko
Kobo Ai
3332-1392 Kami-Sasao,
Kobuchisawa-cho,
Yamanashi Prefecture
0551 36 4361

Watanabe Somemono Ten
Tatemachi
Hachiman-cho,
Gujo-gun,
Gifu Prefecture
0575 65 3959

Yomitan-son Kyodo Hanbai Center
(craft co-op & restaurant)
2723-1 Aza Zakimi,
Yomitan-son, Okinawa
098 958 1020

32 craftsmen, including:

Inamine, Seikichi
(glassmaker)

Omine, Jissei
(potter)

Shimabukuro, Tsunehide
(potter)

Yamada, Shinman
(potter)

Museums

Arimatsu Narumi Shibori Kaikan
60-1 Hashi Higashi
Minami, Arimatsu-cho,
Midori-ku, Nagoya-shi,
Aichi Prefecture
052 621 0111

Kurita Museum
2-17-9 Nihonbashi,
Hama-cho,
Chuo-ku, Tokyo
03 3666 6246

Izumo Folk Arts Museum
628 Chiimiya-cho,
Izumo-shi,
Shimane Prefecture
0853 22 6397

Japan Folk Craft Museum
(Mingei-kan)
4-3-33 Komaba,
Meguro-ku, Tokyo
03 3467 4527

Kurashiki Museum of Folk Crafts
1-4-11 Chuo,
Kurashiki-shi,
Okayama Prefecture
0864 22 1637

Matsumoto Folk Craft Museum
1313-1 Shimokanai,
Satoyamabe,
Matsumoto-shi,
Nagano Prefecture
0263 33 1569

Serizawa Keisuke Museum
5-10-5 Toro,
Shizuoka-shi,
Shizuoka Prefecture
0542 82 5522

Suntory Museum
Suntory Bldg. 11Fl.,
1-2-3 Moto Akasaka,
Minato-ku, Tokyo
03 3470 1073

Toguri Museum
1-11-3 Shoto,
Shibuya-ku, Tokyo
03 3465 0070

Toyama Museum
675 Shiroinuma,
Kawajima-machi,
Hiki-gun,
Saitama Prefecture
0492 97 0007

Yuasa Hachiro Museum
International Christian
University,
3-10-2 Osawa,
Mitaka-shi, Tokyo
0422 33 3340

Yufuin Kuso no Mori Art Museum
Torigoe, Yufuin-cho,
Oita-gun,
Oita Prefecture, Kyushu
0977 85 4007

Restaurants

Hiroo Kiraku
Sun Palace Bldg. 1Fl.,
4-2-49 Minami Azabu,
Minato-ku, Tokyo
03 3444 8971

Katsukichi Tonkatsu
Zen Suido Kaikan Bldg.
1-4-1 Hongo
Bunkyo-ku, Tokyo
03 3812 6268

Kisso
Axis Bldg. B1,
5-17-1 Roppongi,
Minato-ku, Tokyo
03 3582 4191

Rêves de Vie Centre Français des Arts
2-12-1 Shiroganedai,
Minato-ku, Tokyo
03 3444 5711

Flea Markets

First Sunday of the month Arai Yakushi
Temple (Arai Yakushiji-mae Station on the
Seibu Shinjuku Line)

First and fourth Sundays Togo Shrine
(Harajuku Station on
the Yamanote Line or
Meiji-Jingumae Station
on the Chiyoda Line)

Second Sunday Nogi
Shrine (Nogizaka
Station on the Chiyoda
Line); Kumagawa
Shrine (Fussa City)

Third Sunday
Hanazono Shrine
(Shinjuku San-chome
Station on the
Marunouchi Line)

Third Sunday
Takahata Fudo,
Hino City,
Tokyo

Third Thursday and Friday of each month
Roi Building (Roppongi
Station on the Hibiya
Line)

Twenty-first of each month, rain or shine
Toji Temple, Kyoto

Twenty-fifth of each month, rain or shine
Kitano Tenjin Shrine,
Kyoto

Twenty-eighth of each month Narita Fudo
Shrine (Kawagoe,
Saitama Prefecture, on
the Tobu Line)

December 15, 16 and January 15, 16
Boro Ichi (Setagaya
Station on the
Setagaya Line)
Tokyo

March, May, June, September, December
Heiwajima Antiques Fair
(Ryutsu Center Station
on the Tokyo Monorail
from Hamamatsucho
Station)

Blue and white vocabulary

Aizome   Indigo dyeing

Arita   Porcelains, blue and white and otherwise, made in Arita, Kyushu

Bangasa   Japanese paper umbrella

Bashofu   Banana-fiber cloth

Daikon   White radish

Furoshiki   Square carrying cloth

Futon   Sleeping quilt

Genkan   Entrance

Hibachi   Brazier for warming the hands

Imari   Porcelains, originally blue and white, named for the port in Kyushu from which they were shipped

Irori   Sunken open hearth

Jimbei   Two-piece cotton suit

Karakusa   Arabesque

Kasuri   Patterned blue and white cloth

Katazome   Stencil dyeing

Kotatsu   Covered foot-warming table

Maneki neko   Figurine of a cat with raised paw (thought to invite prosperity)

Momen   Cotton

Monpe   Baggy cotton work pants, usually *kasuri* and usually for women

Noren   Divided doorway curtain

Noshi   Folded paper (originally abalone) used to decorate a gift

Obi   Sash for kimono

Onigiri   Rice ball

Sakiori   Ragweave

Sashiko   Stitchery designs and reinforcements on cloth, usually indigo

Shibori   Resist dyeing by tying, binding, sewing, or folding cloth to achieve designs

Shimenawa   Sacred New Year's decoration of rice straw and paper

Shishi   Temple dog or lion

Soba choko   Cup used for dipping sauce for buckwheat noodles

Sometsuke   Blue and white underglaze porcelain; design technique used to achieve such porcelain

Tansu   Chest with drawers

Tenugui   Long cotton hand towel with stenciled designs

Tsutsugaki   Freehand design achieved by applying paste resist with a tube applicator before a textile is dyed

Uzumaki   Spiral motif

Washi   Japanese handmade paper

Yogi, yogu   Padded kimono-shaped bedding

Yukata   Kimono-shaped light cotton robe for after the bath and summer wear

Zabuton   Floor cushion